Smithsonian

LITTLE EXPLORER

INSECTS

by Martha E. H. Rustad

CAPSTONE PRESS
a capstone imprint

Little Explorer is published by Capstone Press,
1710 Roe Crest Drive, North Mankato, Minnesota 56003
www.capstonepub.com

Library of Congress Cataloging-in-Publication Data
Rustad, Martha E. H. (Martha Elizabeth Hillman), 1975–
Insects / by Martha E. H. Rustad.
pages cm. — (Smithsonian little explorer. Little scientist)
Summary: "Introduces types of insects to young readers,
including habitat, diet, and life cycle"— Provided by publisher.
Audience: Ages 4–7
Audience: K to grade 3
Includes index.
ISBN 978-1-4914-0792-9 (library binding)
ISBN 978-1-4914-0796-7 (paperback)
ISBN 978-1-4914-0794-3 (paper over board)
ISBN 978-1-4914-0798-1 (eBook PDF)
1. Insects—Juvenile literature. I. Title.
QL467.2.R875 2015
595.7—dc23   2014000193

Editorial Credits
Michelle Hasselius, editor; Sarah Bennett, designer; Kelly Garvin,
media researcher; Tori Abraham, production specialist

Our very special thanks to Alan Peters, Curator, Invertebrate
Exhibit and Pollinarium; Michael Miller, Animal Keeper,
Invertebrate Exhibit and Pollinarium; Donna Stockton, Animal
Keeper, Invertebrate Exhibit and Pollinarium; and Jennifer Zoon,
Communications Assistant at Smithsonian's National Zoological
Park for their review. Capstone would also like to thank Kealy
Wilson, Smithsonian Institution Product Development Manager,
and the following at Smithsonian Enterprises: Ellen Nanney,
Licensing Manager; Brigid Ferraro, Vice President, Education and
Consumer Products; and Carol LeBlanc, Senior Vice President,
Education and Consumer Products.

Image Credits
Alamy: Harold Gough/PBPA, 8 (top), Scott Camazine, 13
(bottom); Dreamstime/Mauhorng, 20-21; Minden Pictures/
Mitsuhiko Imamori/Nature Production, 9 (top); Shutterstock:
24 Novembers, 18, alexsvirid, 26-27, Aliaksandr Radzko, insect
art, Amir Ridhwan, 25, Andrei Nekrassov, 12 (bottom), Andrey
Pavlov, 11 (bottom), Arto Hakola, 8 (bottom), Barnaby Chambers,
21 (bottom), biker11, 10 (bottom), ChinellatoPhoto, 6, cynoclub,
7 (middle), D. Kucharski Kucharska, 8 (bottom), Dean Fikar, 18
(bottom), Dirk Ercken, 23 (top), Dmitri Gomon, 11 (middle), 14
(top), Dr. Morley Read, 4 (top), eKawatchaow, 12 (top), Henrik
Larsson, 4 (bottom), Jeff McGraw, 19 (right), Joseph Calev, 16
(middle), Kamnuan, 7 (bottom), Kirsanov Valeriy Vladimirovich,
5, 29 (middle), Lakeview Images, 13, 30-31, Lehrer, 15 (top),
Lobke Peers, 22, Matee Nuserm, 19 (left), mchin, 26, (bottom),
Mirek Kijewski, 28-29, mrfiza, 3, Paul Bowling, 15 (bottom), Peter
Schwarz, 10 (top), Potapov Alexander, insect art, ROmacho, 23
(bottom), Snookless, 7 (top), Souchon Yves, 9 (top), Steve Cukrov,
14 (bottom), sydeen, 11 (top), Thumbelina, insect art, Tuckraider,
cover, Vitalii Hulai, 9 (middle), yanikap, 17, Yuangeng Zhang,
1, 32; Superstock: Belinda Images, 28 (bottom), Biosphoto, 9
(bottom), 15 (middle), 24 (bottom), FLPA, 24, Mark Cassino, 16
(bottom), Minden Pictures, 16 (top), 25 (bottom)

For Emerson Amelia, Caroline Grace, and Anabelle Elise.—MEHR

Printed in the United States of America in Stevens Point, Wisconsin.
032014   008092WZF14

TABLE OF CONTENTS

LOOK AROUND FOR INSECTS

Insects live everywhere. In the air, in the water, on the ground, and in the dirt.

Take a look around you. Find an insect.

Have you seen an insect sitting in the sun? Insects are cold-blooded. The sunlight warms their bodies.

AN INSECT'S BODY

An insect is an animal with three body sections.

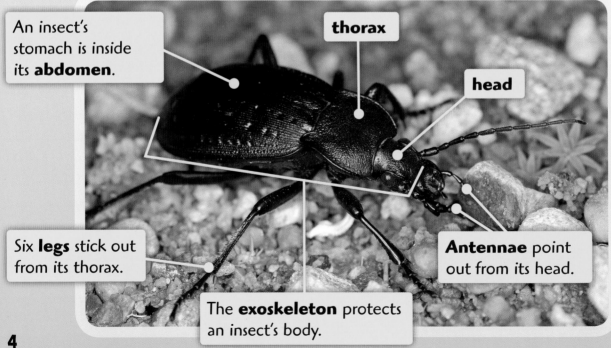

An insect's stomach is inside its **abdomen**.

thorax

head

Six **legs** stick out from its thorax.

Antennae point out from its head.

The **exoskeleton** protects an insect's body.

The world contains more insects than any other animal. Scientists have found more than 1 million kinds of insects. They expect to find more.

ANCIENT INSECTS

Earth has been home to insects for a long time. Scientists have found insect fossils that are millions of years old.

Many ancient insects looked like insects today. But some ancient insects were big. Their wings stretched as wide as 2.5 feet (76.2 centimeters).

a fossil of a midge insect

Imagine an insect as wide as a school desk!

WHAT IS **NOT** AN INSECT?

People call lots of animals bugs. But many are **not** insects.

SPIDERS are not insects. Spiders have two body sections and eight legs.

TICKS are not insects. Eight legs stick out from their bodies.

MILLIPEDES are not insects. They crawl on as many as 400 legs!

METAMORPHOSIS

An insect's body changes as it grows.
Most insects go through four changes.
These changes are called metamorphosis.

Here is the metamorphosis of a
seven-spotted lady beetle.

1

larva

eggs

The seven-spotted lady beetle
begins as an egg. The larva
hatches from the egg. Larvae
look like tiny worms.

2

larva

The larva eats and
grows. It molts
when it outgrows
its exoskeleton.
Molt means to shed
its outer covering.

pupa

The larva molts into a pupa. Inside, its body changes. The adult beetle breaks out of the pupa.

dragonfly nymph

Some insects, such as grasshoppers and dragonflies, go through only three stages—egg, nymph, and adult. A nymph looks like a small adult.

adult

A female adult mates and lays eggs. The life cycle begins again.

INSECT SENSES

SEEING

Most adult insects see the world through different types of eyes.

Tiny single eyes see light and dark. Huge compound eyes have many small lenses. Each lens sees a different part of the picture.

One compound eye of a dragonfly may have 28,000 lenses!

HEARING

Most insects hear well. Some gather sounds with round ears called tympana. Others use hairs on their antennae to hear.

TOUCHING

Insects feel with tiny strands that look like hair.

TASTING AND SMELLING

Many insects use the strands on their antennae for smelling and tasting. Some insects even have them on their feet!

SENSING CHEMICALS

These strands also sense chemicals. Chemicals help insects communicate. They use chemicals to find mates and food.

ANTS

Ants work. Each ant has a different job.

The queen lays eggs. Worker ants feed young ants and build nests. Soldier ants protect the nest.

Ant colonies live in nests. One nest might be home to a million ants.

A troop of ants work together to move a fly.

ant nest made of wood

Ants build nests from dirt, leaves, or wood.

An ant colony has one queen. But sometimes a colony makes new queens. They fly off to start new ant colonies.

BEES

Bees buzz. They gather nectar and pollen from flowers.

Some kinds of bees live in large colonies.

Hives may have up to 80,000 bees. Adults take care of young bees.

Other kinds of bees live
alone. They lay eggs in
nests. The bees leave
food for their young.
Then they leave the nest.

Some bees
have stingers.
They sting to
protect their
hive. Not all
bees sting.

Honeybees collect nectar in
honeycombs. Mixed with a
bee's saliva, nectar turns into
honey as it dries.

carpenter bee

An insect's egg can be smaller than a
period on this page. One of the largest
insect eggs belongs to the carpenter bee.
It is 0.64 inches (1.6 cm) long.

BEETLES

Beetles battle.
Rhinoceros beetles
fight over food
and mates.

Ladybugs gobble.
They are also called
ladybird beetles. Most
ladybugs eat other
insects called aphids.

Fireflies flash. The lights
on these beetles signal
other fireflies.

Four wings stick out from most beetles. Two hard top wings protect a beetle's two soft bottom wings. Beetles fly with the two bottom wings.

There are about 360,000 kinds of beetles.

BUTTERFLIES AND MOTHS

Moths and butterflies flutter by. Strong muscles power delicate wings. Colorful scales cover their wings.

Butterflies and moths suck plant juices with a proboscis. This mouthpart looks like a straw.

BUTTERFLY OR MOTH?

Here are some ways to tell the difference between a butterfly and a moth.

Butterflies	Moths
bright colors	dull colors
knob on the end of each antenna	feathery antennae
wings held up to rest	wings held out to rest
awake in the day	awake at night
molt into chrysalis	spin cocoon

Some moths and butterflies break these rules. There are butterflies with dull-colored wings and moths that are awake in the day.

COCKROACHES

Cockroaches scurry. They hide during the day. At night they come out to eat. Cockroaches run away fast if they sense danger.

Cockroaches often
live near people.
Food crumbs, clothes,
and paper taste good to them.

TOUGH PESTS

A cockroach can live up to a
month without food. It can live
two weeks without water. It can
even live without its head for
up to a week!

DRAGONFLIES

Dragonflies zoom up and down. They even hover and fly backward.

Their strong jaws chomp insect snacks in midair, but adult dragonflies don't bite people.

Dragonflies live near water.
Female dragonflies lay eggs
in or near water.

Young dragonflies
live underwater.
They breathe
with gills.

FLIES

Flies fly. A fly buzzes around on two wings. Scientists think sticky feet help flies walk on ceilings.

Flies eat only liquids. They spit up their solid food. Then they suck it back up as liquid.

Mosquitoes are a kind of fly.
They often bother people.

Females drink blood from
people and other
animals. Their eggs
need blood
to grow.

"If you think you are too small to make a difference,
you haven't spent a night with a mosquito."
—African proverb

Female flies lay hundreds of eggs in their short lives.

25

GRASSHOPPERS

Grasshoppers hop. Long legs push them high and far. Wings sometimes help them go even farther.

Grasshoppers chomp. They eat many different plants.

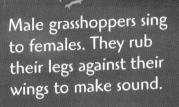

Male grasshoppers sing to females. They rub their legs against their wings to make sound.

INSECTS AND HUMANS

Insects sometimes hurt people. Flies spread diseases. Swarms of grasshoppers eat crops.

But insects also help us. Bees move pollen from one flower to another. Without their help, many plants could not grow.

Beetles break down dead plants. They help make soil rich again.

Insects outnumber humans. Scientists think for each human, there are 200 million insects!

We must live together and share this planet.

GLOSSARY

abdomen—the back section of an insect's body

ancient—from a long time ago

antennae—feelers on an insect's head; insects use antennae to sense movement

aphid—an insect that sucks plant juices

chemical—a substance insects use to communicate

chrysalis—a hard shell where a butterfly pupa changes into an adult

cocoon—a covering made of silky threads; a moth makes a cocoon to protect itself while it changes from larva to pupa

cold-blooded—having a body that needs to get heat from its surroundings

colony—a large group of animals that live and work together

compound eyes—made up of lots of lenses; they are good for seeing fast-moving things

exoskeleton—a hard outer covering on an animal

fossil—the remains or traces of an animal or a plant, preserved as rock

gill—a body part some insects use to breathe underwater

hive—a place where a group of bees lives

hover—to stay in one place in the air

larva—the second life stage of an insect; more than one larva are called larvae

lens—a clear part of the eye that helps you see objects clearly

mate—to join together to produce young; a mate is also the male or female partner of a pair of animals

metamorphosis—the series of changes some animals go through as they develop from eggs to adults

nectar—a sweet liquid that some insects collect from flowers and eat as food

nymph—a young form of an insect; nymphs change into adults by shedding their exoskeleton many times

pollen—tiny, yellow grains in flowers

proboscis—a long, tube-shaped mouthpart; insects use this to drink plant juices

pupa—an insect at the life stage between a larva and an adult

saliva—clear liquid in an animal's mouth

thorax—the middle section of an insect's body; wings and legs are attached to it

tympana—parts of an insect's body that gather sounds

CRITICAL THINKING USING THE COMMON CORE

Turn to page 5. What is the person in the photo doing? What clues did you use from the photo to help you with your answer? (Key Ideas and Details)

Read the African proverb on page 25. What do you think it means? What can a mosquito do to you even though it's much smaller in size? (Craft and Structure)

Go outside and find an insect. What type of insect is it? How do you know this? Use the text to help you with your answer. (Integration of Knowledge and Ideas)

READ MORE

Levy, Janey. *Tiny Bugs Up Close.* Under the Microscope. New York: Gareth Stevens Pub., 2014.

Veitch, Catherine. *Learning About Insects.* The Natural World. Chicago: Raintree, 2014.

Voake, Steve. *Insect Detective.* Somerville, Mass.: Candlewick Press, 2010.

INTERNET SITES

FactHound offers a safe, fun way to find Internet sites related to this book. All of the sites on FactHound have been researched by our staff.

Here's all you do:

Visit *www.facthound.com*

Type in this code: 9781491407929

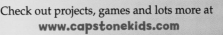
Super-cool stuff! Check out projects, games and lots more at
www.capstonekids.com

INDEX